Happy is the New Rich

(and 207 Other Lightbulb Moments)

BY GEORGE RESCH

Published by Tank.Sinatra Press
All Rights Reserved. Print Edition number 1

B. C. Allen Publishing and Tonic Books
1500 SE Hawthorne Blvd.
Portland, OR, 97214
Now taking manuscript submissions
and book ideas at any stage of the process
bcallenpublishingsubmissions@gmail.com

Cover Design (Adam Padilla)
Interior Design (Dave Bryant)
Design overseen by the Author, George Resch

ISBN: 978-0-9968551-4-3

To my wife Jessica, without whose love and support this book would never have materialized.

Introduction

I wrote this book over the course of ten years, while struggling with and overcoming every issue a quasi-adult might face. (A quasi-adult is when you're still an idiot but you have bills and responsibilities.) The majority of the material in this book originated in my mind, but there are a handful of thoughts that I picked up along the way that are universal truths, without any single place of origin. They were helpful to me, so I put them in here to help you.

This book is for anybody who feels like they're not where they want to be in life, for anyone who feels like something is missing, and for anyone who feels like they weren't given the "Manual for Living" that everyone else seems to have.

I recommend skimming the pages to get a feel for the material, and leaving any expectations for the book aside. Let the material speak to you when it's appropriate. If you don't understand something, don't worry. It may make sense at a later date, as your life unfolds. Just know that you aren't meant to relate to every piece of content in this book.

As a matter of fact, if you relate to everything in this book, your life probably sucks as badly as mine did, and I'm sorry. There is no practical guide or three-step program to developing self-awareness, but this book grew out of my own hard-earned self-awareness, and my hope is that it helps you find yours.

D0978365

A life free of mistakes
is a life half-lived.

The best way to get smart
is to get well-acquainted
with looking stupid.

Be short with difficult problems,
and patient with difficult people.

Free time is only valuable when you don't have any.

One guaranteed way to make absolutely sure you do not do something is to set out to do it perfectly the first time.

If you're going to learn
everything the hard way,
at least learn the
lesson *permanently.*
Don't be a hard learner
and an easy forgetter.

Just because you don't like the way things turned out doesn't mean that something went wrong. The only thing wrong with your past is the way you perceive it.

Action without thought
creates havoc.
Thought without action
creates anxiety.
Make thought and action equal
partners, while cutting talk
out of the deal completely.

Fantasizing will give you pleasure,
but action will give you joy.

If you're such a control freak,
    why don't you use some of that
control to control yourself so you
    can stop trying to control me?

Happiness is a choice,
not a transaction.

You can bury the pain if you want. Just know that pain always gets buried alive.

Your *self-worth* should not be determined by your *net worth.*

Difficulty lies in the future
and vanishes in the present.

My idea of hell is when I feel bad
but *not* bad enough
to do anything about it.

Perfectionism and procrastination are both paralyzing and can only be solved by one thing:

action.

There's a big difference between making sure your needs are met and being needy.
Don't be afraid to tell people what you need so you can feel happy, safe, and secure in a relationship, whether it be personal or professional.

Treat everyone in your inner circle as though they're an invited guest to the party of your life.

You're the one that invited them, whether you meant to or not.

You do have control over
who you let into your life.
You do not have control over what
they do once they get there.

Procrastination
is stillborn perfectionism.

Don't let other people succeed
at keeping you from succeeding.

The more I act the way I need to,
the less I need you to act the
way I think you should.

Most people give the world at large their very best, and give whatever's left over to their friends and family. I do the opposite, and tomorrow I want you to try it too. Don't hold the door open for some random person then not open the car door for your wife of 15 years. Hasn't she earned better treatment than a stranger?

I try to be on my best behavior with friends and family and give whatever is left over to the strangers of the world. The big surprise here is that being kind to the people that are close to you is energizing and invigorating, and it puts you in a better position to be kind to everybody else you come across. On the flip side, putting on a fake happy face for strangers leaves you exhausted and ill-equipped to be loving with the people who matter to you most.

If you're going to do
something out of character,
try to have it *raise* the
standard of your behavior
rather than *lowering* it.

Be less concerned with how
your actions affect others,
and more concerned with
how they affect you.
If something makes you feel bad or
guilty, lowers your self-worth, or is
just not a reflection of the kind of
person you want to be, then stop.

That's it. Just don't do it.

God
is not a painkiller.

Let go of *"what if"*
and hold onto *"what is."*

Entitlement
is our generation's epidemic.

You know you're emotionally
healthy when, in the heat
of the moment, you can
take your own advice.

> If you can do what you'd tell
> somebody else to do if they
> were in your situation, you
> are a true champion at life.

Trust your instincts.
They'll never lie to you;
they don't know how.
Your mind handles that.

Let's be honest, most people can't handle being right during an argument.
If you're wrong, keep your mouth shut.
If you're right, keep your mouth shut *a little tighter*.

Being a perfectionist is knowing that something isn't good enough before you've even begun.

Change your plan as frequently as you need to; change your purpose rarely, if ever.

Money only solves one problem:
the money problem.

If you want to be in a
healthy relationship,
   don't look for the right person.
            Be the right person.

It's better to do the right
thing for the wrong reasons
than to do the wrong thing
for the right reasons.
You will be judged by your
actions, not your intentions.

Tomorrow never comes.
As long as today is today,
tomorrow is a mirage.
Some people use the promise of a
better tomorrow as a way to hold
on to hope, but the majority of
people use the idea of tomorrow
as fuel to never do anything today.

When people share a piece of themselves or their history with you, use it to understand them, not to judge them or hold it against them in future arguments.

I want to get better at stuff I'm not immediately good at.
I'm not that good at getting better at stuff I'm not so good at right away.
If I'm not good at something naturally on the first try, I tend to want to not do it at all.

Good rule of thumb
(pun so intended):
Don't text or email anything you
wouldn't say with your mouth,
in person or on the phone.
Don't let the barrier of a
screen make you act bolder
than you normally do.
Just because you're not "saying
it" doesn't mean you're not
saying it. As a matter of fact,
it's worse. It's in writing, and
some writing doesn't erase.

Some people spend time
alone so they don't have to
spend time with others.
Some people spend time with
others so they don't have to
spend time with themselves.
There's gotta be a happy
medium in there somewhere.

Find it.

Mind over matter.

Spirit over mind.

When it comes to a
blossoming relationship,
don't paint red flags green.
Red flags are red flags.
You don't have to bolt as soon
as you see one, but take it
as a sign to slow down and
proceed with caution. *Don't
pretend you didn't see it.*

I'm a very sensitive person.
I always have been and I
probably always will be.
   I thank God for my sensitivity
      because it allows me to feel
         tremendous gratitude.
            If I had not felt all that pain
               and embarrassment in the
                  past, I might not appreciate
                     the absence of it today.

Happiness is not a result of luck
or an accumulation of material shit.
People that are happy don't
belong to some exclusive club.
Happiness is available to those
who realize that happiness is a
byproduct of love and service.

The better we get,
the sicker we think we are.

In theory, it's easy to adopt new ideals and standards for behavior, but it's a lot harder to put those behaviors into practice consistently so that you can walk the walk you're trying to talk.

Life is a gentle teacher.
It'll keep pushing you in
the direction of the mistake
you're making until you
learn your lesson.

Sometimes, it feels like the
whole world and all its people
are working against you.

Know in your heart that
life is not an adversary.

Life is a professor.

You're living the life that
you choose. Sometimes
this is a compliment; other
times it's an insult.
   Sometimes it's a pat on the back;
   other times it's a kick in the ass.
            But it's always the truth.

Greed tells you that you'll never have enough, even though you have more than you'll ever need.
Learn to have enough.

W hen people first start dating there's always the question of how long to wait until the first time they have sex. My philosophy is that it's different with every couple. Some people wait zero days, while some wait a month, or until marriage, and neither approach is wrong. What's wrong is placing an arbitrary waiting period on intimacy. Here's why I don't have sex with somebody right away. The time between the moment you meet and the first time you have sex is absolute fucking magic (pun intended). You don't get a second chance to feel that insane amount of sexual tension with that person, so why not drag it out as long as you can? If you can only wait four hours, good for you. If you can wait a month, good for you, too. Just wait as long as you can, not to prove a point, but to enjoy the process.

I really do have a
great life on paper.
It's amazing, though,
how I sometimes become
completely illiterate.

People who get everything they want are never as happy as people who want everything they have.

Don't wish for more money; wish for freedom from financial insecurity.
Don't focus on finding the right person; focus on being the right person.
Don't put all the emphasis on losing weight; work to cultivate a positive self-image.

Why do people try to keep
their loved ones from making
the same mistakes they made?
Isn't that how they got
all their wisdom?
The growth is in the lessons
learned through pain, not
the avoidance of failure.

Lust makes you pretend
problems don't exist;
      love lets you accept that they do.

Life is full of disappointments,
especially when you place
unrealistic demands on yourself
and the world around you.
Not every disappointment has
to be a devastation, though.
Try to feel an appropriate
amount of letdown.
Let the punishment fit the crime.

It's easier to keep up
than it is to catch up.
This goes for cleaning your
room, maintenance on your
car, communication with
your spouse, your weight,
your homework, your bills,
everything.

Exercise is not a punishment,
it's a gift.

Life is a bumpy road, so you need to learn to enjoy the ride. Buckle up.

Of course life is full of ups and downs. It's supposed to be. When it's a flatline, you're dead.

Acceptance doesn't mean approval.
You can't change people, and you can't change certain circumstances, which means you have to eat shit sometimes. But that doesn't mean you have to approve of it.
It just means you don't have to fight life every step of the way.

People *listen* to wisdom,
but they *obey* pain.

Quantity of time is the
way to quality time.
Quality time doesn't happen if
you're not around enough to
allow moments to happen.
The biggest lie people tell
themselves is that they can spend
almost no time with their loved
ones, and still get the high-quality
moments they're looking for.
The more you're around, the
more opportunity you give life
to provide you with memories
that you'll never forget.

Doubt your doubt.
Have faith in your faith.

The A.R.T. of living
is to
Always Remain Teachable.

I can either ask questions and
look stupid now,
                or assume and
                        look stupid later.

It's impossible for a problem
to exist without a solution.
It's like dark existing without light.
You wouldn't recognize one
from the other unless they were
both pieces of the puzzle.

Time and pressure are inversely proportional in most situations. The lesser one gets, the greater the other becomes. (Which is why most of us wait like idiots until the last minute to do everything, especially writing papers.)

Like the ocean, life is going where it's going whether you like it or not. You can either dive under, get tumbled, or learn how to surf.

I don't have all the answers,
and I don't trust people
who think they do.
　　　If you really want to amass as
　　　much knowledge as you can
　　　in this lifetime, forget about
　　　knowing all the answers.
　　　Practice and perfect the art of
　　　asking the right questions.

Life is not a race.
It's definitely one thing you
don't want to finish first.

Hope is for the future.
Faith is for the present.
Acceptance is for the past.
People often practice the exact opposite. They're fearful about the future, doubtful about the present, and full of regret about their past.

Everybody likes validation. We just have to determine which sources of validation are healthy and which are not. Sharing mundane details of my life constantly for likes from strangers on the internet is a world apart from sharing good news with a close friend.

I've found it's important
to have dreams,
but it's vital to make decisions.

I don't get frustrated when
people make mistakes.
I get frustrated when
people make excuses.

Don't help people if you're going to be looking for something in return.

Being kind is its own reward.

However, if I hold the door for you and you don't say thank you, I want to slam the door in your face. That's, like, one exception.

Don't compare your insides with other people's outsides.

When I first moved to California, I couldn't believe how rich everybody was, or appeared to be. One night in particular, I was feeling very down about my financial situation. I was at my friend Jason's house, when his friend Nick pulled up in a brand new Porsche. My heart sank. I immediately felt like less of a man than him. Where was my nice car? As the car door opened, a tall, handsome dude with a suit and full head of hair emerged. He walked around the car and opened the passenger door, which revealed a gorgeous young blonde, with big fake boobs and a tight miniskirt. I was so fucking envious of this guy, you have no idea. As we got ready to leave, I saw Nick pull Jason to the side. Nick told Jason that he had to drive because Nick had no money to put gas in the car. He also informed Jason he would need to park the Porsche in the garage because the bank was looking to repossess the vehicle. It was at that moment I vowed two things: never compare myself to somebody else's appearance, and never work that hard to keep up my own.

The fact that you're even alive and able to complain should be enough to make you want to stop complaining.

When I say "I can't,"
what I'm really saying
is "I don't want to."

It takes a lot of discipline
to wake up early,
but it takes even more
to go to bed early.

Actions speak louder than words,
but underlying motives
speak volumes.

What willpower can't
control, a higher power can.
If you're having a particularly
tough time cutting out a
compulsive destructive behavior,
ask God, or whatever you
believe in (as long as it's not
yourself) for help with it.
It can't hurt.

Science is man's best attempt
to explain all that is seen and
objectively observable.
Spirituality is man's best attempt
to explain all that is unseen and
only subjectively observable.
Unfortunately, you can't measure
spiritual experiences, but that
doesn't mean they're not real.

Don't believe in science more than spirituality. The way science worshippers act they'd have you thinking that man actually invented the heart. We didn't, we just figured it out . . . kind of.

Don't waste wishes on your past, just make plans for the future. In other words, don't wish things went differently last time, use what you learned to make sure they go differently this time.

Try to live in a more manageable range of emotions. Don't be afraid to feel, but keep the highs below manic, and the lows above suicidal. Remember to allow the event or circumstances to evoke the right amount of emotion: a text back from your crush shouldn't feel like the birth of a child, and a bad grade isn't a cancer diagnosis.

What you do not have
control over: outcome.

What you do have
control over: outlook.

The only way for a person
to become deep is to
continue to dig for truth.

Don't hold in your best
and let out your worst.
Be mindful of what
you show the world.

They say if you change
too much in a relationship
to please somebody you'll
wind up resenting them,
but there's a big difference between
your partner asking you to watch a
movie you don't want to watch and
your partner demanding that you
stop being emotionally abusive.

Stop focusing so much
on losing weight,
and start focusing on
building self-esteem.

Watch your ego.
When the ego is swollen,
each bump in the road feels
like a personal attack, like it's
happening directly to you,
instead of just happening as part
of the normal life process.
The smallest disappointment or
inconvenience makes you feel
like you're being punished by
life, instead of being grateful that
you're alive long enough to have
a lot happen—good and bad.

When given direction
or constructive criticism,
emotionally healthy people say
"okay" more than "I know."
   If you're doing something wrong
   and somebody tells you and you
       say "I know," then why didn't
       you do that in the first place?
       Because you didn't know.
                        Just say "okay."

It's important for me
to be convinced of my
convictions, not you.
You can tell how insecure someone
is in their beliefs by how hard
they push them on other people.

I am done letting my emotions determine my actions. You know who acts how they feel? Babies and animals.

Try the opposite, and let your actions dictate your feelings. Sometimes you have to act how you want to feel so that you can feel how you want to.

You want to feel happy?
Act happy.

You want to feel helpful?
Act helpful.

You want to feel loving?
Love.

Drugs, alcohol, eating, and sex can all act as void-filling behaviors and emotional crutches. When you use them to try and deal with how you're feeling and go around in pain instead of growing through it, you stifle your development. You stunt your emotional and spiritual growth.

I have be careful not to get wrapped up in good intentions.

When I think about or talk about my good intentions, most of the time I feel so good I don't even have to do what I intended to do. I already got the emotional reward.

Take this for example: you proclaim "I'm going to the gym, tomorrow! Definitely!"

Tomorrow arrives and you never get off the couch because, why would you? You already got that shot of dopamine from mentally going to the gym yesterday, and you didn't even have to lift a finger, let alone a dumbbell. Life isn't about feelings. You don't remember feelings, you remember experiences.

Check your motives.

If you're demanding any type of result from an action you're taking, you're not coming from the right place. You're most likely being selfish, rather than selfless. Go back and figure out what you're trying to accomplish (approval or an owed favor, for example) and instead of taking the roundabout approach, go direct. In other words, be loving for the sake of being loving.

Don't get mad at
collection agencies.
They're not harassing you
to get *your* money.
They're harassing you
to get *their* money.

Honesty without compassion is cruelty. Thoughts can't be heard, but words can, and once they're out there, they can't be taken back. Don't think you're doing your loved ones any favors by telling them what's wrong with them day in and day out. They already know, and they're working on it with whatever tools they have at their disposal. If you really want to help somebody, give them new tools, not the same information over and over again. People learn by example and observation.

Perfectionism is just procrastination with a slightly better track record; perfectionism is fear of not doing it perfectly, while procrastination is fear of doing it, period.

When it comes to dealing with a difficult significant other, keep this thought in mind: I am not the repairman and I am not a mind-reader.

Next time somebody is venting to you about something in their life, just listen. Don't fix them or dismiss them because you think you know their problem and their solution better than they do. Sometimes people just want to be heard and have a safe forum to speak openly and honestly, which can help them get the answers from themselves.

If you're offering advice,
make sure there is a genuine
desire to help the suffering person
and you're not just giving them
a solution so you don't have
to listen to them anymore.

Question everything you know,
especially the stuff you're
100% certain about.

Many people say that anger is just another expression of fear, and for me, anger is fear's final form. But for some, it's the first and only way their fear comes out. Most people don't anger easily. They can be bothered without getting angry right away.

When somebody angers quickly and easily, *that's a red flag,* especially in the beginning of a relationship when everybody is on their best behavior. If that's your best behavior, I'm not sticking around to see what your worst is like.

Delay showing anyone your angry, ugly face for as long as possible. Once yelling and name-calling is established as acceptable behavior, it's a hard habit to break. It's much more difficult to keep your cool in the midst of an argument, but it's infinitely more rewarding. I should know, I kept my mouth shut once. *It was amazing.*

Love is an action.
Love is a choice to take
loving action even in
the face of frustration,
disappointment, or betrayal.

When I talk shit about myself, don't agree with me, even if you do.

If you do agree, say nothing. If you don't agree with what I'm doing or what I say about myself, let me know. There's a good chance I'm looking at life through cloudy glasses, rather than fishing for compliments.

Only God can judge me, but he won't, so what's your problem? How could you judge me when you've lived as imperfectly as I have? Just because you've made different mistakes than me doesn't give you the right to judge the ones I've made.

Ever heard somebody utter this nonsense: "He's a good guy deep down"?

My response to that bullshit statement: "How deep are we talking here?" When was the last time he showed you something worth sticking around for?

You might look at me and think I've never had a problem in my life. That is not the case. I've had every problem imaginable.

It's like the color white. You're not looking at the absence of color, you're looking at every color together. The people who have lived through the most pain tend to shine the brightest and reflect the most beauty, like a prism.

Just because I disagree with you doesn't mean I dislike you. And I don't think you're stupid just because I have an abundance of information in one area that I've taken an interest in and you haven't. It means you haven't immersed yourself in it yet, which is fine.

There are a lot of topics I have no knowledge of and can't speak intelligently about. That doesn't mean I'm dumb. *It means I haven't gotten to it yet.*

I'm not perfect, *but my life is.* Pain is not caused by the fact that your life is imperfect. It occurs when you fight the fact that your life is perfect right now, even though it's not the way you think it *should* be. I can't tell you how many times I didn't get my way and it wound up turning out *way better* than the plan I had.

Pain is a great motivator;
    it'll get you in motion.
        But action and goals will
            keep you going.

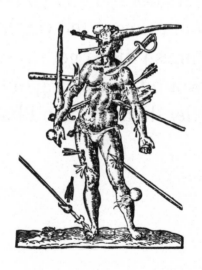

You never have a
reason to worry.
Always ask yourself,
"Is there anything I can
do about this right now?"
If the answer is no,
then don't stress.
If the answer is yes, then do what
you can, but still don't stress.

Just act.

Being a character is
doing what's wrong when
everybody is watching.

Having character is doing
what's right even when
nobody is watching.

Help the people around
you become the people
they want to become,
not the people *you* want
them to become.

It's amazing how the only
people I want to change for
are the ones who fully accept
me and take me as I am.

You're not in traffic;
you are traffic.
The same can be said when people
blame society for their problems.
Stop putting off ownership.
You are society.

Asking somebody to compromise on their preferences is a lot different than asking them to *violate their conscience.*

Don't obsess about
every individual shitty
character trait you have.
Instead, take a step back
and look at your actions.
If they're not in your best
interest, don't do them.
It's harder than it sounds,
but a lot easier than judging
yourself all day and questioning
yourself every step of the way.

Trust yourself to act in
your own interest, and let
life unfold in front of you
as it will, *whether you like it or not.*

Go to people for support,
not approval.
You can bounce a troubling
situation off a good friend and not
get the answer you're looking for.
Let's admit it, *sometimes
you're just wrong.*
A good friend will support
you and be there for you while
still giving it to you straight.

Don't ask a question while holding in your mind the answer you want to hear (or don't want to hear).

That's when inquisitive becomes accusatory, and that tone comes through more than you realize.

Life is short and life is hard.
Ask questions, pay attention, and
use the answers you get, whether
they come directly from people
or by way of life experiences.
If that doesn't work, keep asking
and keep applying until you figure
out what you need to know to
move on to the next lesson.

Opinions and thoughts
are meant to be shared,

not shoved.

Stop trying to be different
for the sake of being different
and just be yourself.

Now that would be unique.

The more I isolate,
the more unique I become.

The more people you meet, *the smaller your world becomes.* If you find yourself saying "it's a small world" a lot, it's not that the world is small, but that *you're a big personality.*

You can only be upset by
somebody's opinion of you if
you care what they think.
    You're only able to care what
        people think of you if you
            need their approval.
        You only need their approval
            if you don't have your own.

Having a big ego with low self-esteem means that everybody is talking about you, *and nobody is saying anything good.*

It's amazing what you'll
believe when you want to
and what you *won't* believe
when you *can't*.

When you love yourself,
having somebody else love
you is like finding a wad of
cash in an old winter jacket.
When you don't love yourself,
having somebody love
you is like trying to pay
bills with sofa change.

Would you wish away your last hundred dollars?

"Man, I wish I could just get rid of this hundred bucks! It's driving me nuts!"

That doesn't make much sense, now does it? It makes even less sense to wish away something infinitely more valuable, like time.

"I wish this day would just end already."

Really?

What if it's your last?

I'm not thankful
because I'm happy.
I'm happy because I'm thankful.

Let go of the need to know
and learn how to live by
going with the flow.

My best relationships
consist of moments when
what you need to say collides
with what I need to hear,
  and when what I need to say is
  the one thing you need to hear.

Live a life based on
principles, not conditions.
Conditions are ever-changing, but
principles should be set in stone.
Live life *un*conditionally.

The reason it's important to have space in a healthy relationship and live full and separate lives is that it gives you something to talk about.
I always thought people wanted space so they could fuck other people.
They just wanted to have a cup of coffee alone.

The only way for me to avoid not getting my way is to not have a way to not get.

Prayer is not so much wishful thinking as it is wishful action.

It's easy to be enlightened when you're basking in the sunlight of good fortune.

The true test of faith and enlightenment is how *brightly* you shine when things are the *darkest* they've ever been.

"Over there" and "right here" are really the same.
The grass isn't greener on the other side.
The grass is greenest where it's watered.

I used to think character
defects were the things I
beat myself up about.
 Then I realized that beating myself
  up is my biggest character defect.

The mistake is not the mistake. The mistake is not changing your behavior and feeling the same pain over and over again.

We must master the
art of staying positive
in a world where negativity
is rewarded.

The hardest part about
knowing what you want to
be when you grow up
 is knowing when you've grown up.

Stop missing people
when they're gone
    and start appreciating them
      while they're still around.

I'd rather force myself to be happy than naturally sad. *Some things are worth a little effort.*

Anything or anybody
that runs your life
       also has the potential to ruin it.

Science does not cancel
out spirituality.
We have to introduce them
and make them fall in love.

A positive outlook can turn a *rut* into a *groove.*

It's funny how the people that can't wait for tomorrow are usually busy enjoying today, while the people who can't wait for today to be over are usually living in yesterday.

Isn't it ironic how money cheapens things?

I'll be comfortable when I'm dead.

They say that misery
loves company.
           Well, guess what?
                  Joy loves company too.

I once heard a woman talking
about another woman she
didn't like because the other
woman "was always talking
shit about everybody when
they weren't around."
Guess what?
The woman she was talking
about wasn't there.
The irony hit me like a truck,
but it completely missed her.

How do you defend against arbitrary skepticism and negativity from others?
    With unbridled passion and
        enthusiasm from within.

The trick is to get comfortable being uncomfortable.
Trust me, it happens.

The best sleeping pill is a
good day's living.

Change means something new is coming more than it means something old is going. When you look at change as an opportunity rather than a loss, it kinda takes the sting out of it.

We all know that life can
take a turn for the worse
in the blink of an eye,
but the same thing happens
for positive change.
Hang tight for those moments.

Nobody is healthy enough to
be in an unhealthy relationship.
Toxic people will ruin you
way before you fix them.

It's amazing what happens when you let your feelings pass through you.

They come and go so quickly. Stop trying to talk the pain away or communicate to the point where you're finally tired of hearing yourself talk about it. That's not relief, *that's exhaustion.* It's good to understand what you're feeling, but it's better to feel what you're feeling and let it pass.

Don't use words to figure out how you feel. *They're just labels.* Use words to describe what you've discovered once you sit in the feeling for a little while. Figure out exactly what it is you're feeling first, then use your vocabulary to describe what you find, whether in a journal or to a person you trust.

Pain is designed to be uncomfortable. You're supposed to try and escape it. The trick is to escape it through healthy avenues.

If you're in pain, ask a few questions, get a few answers. Apply those answers to your life, take some action, and watch the pain dissipate. Instead of searching frantically for a solution, be still and let the solution come to you.

What other people think of
you is none of your business.
They're thinking about what
you think of them just as
much as you're thinking
about what they think of you.
Let's just all agree to cut this
bullshit out once and for all.

Don't compare your insides with other people's outsides.

If we all stood in a circle and threw our collective problems into a pile in the middle, we'd all be clawing to have our own problems back. It's not a great tool to compare your life to how bad it could be, but when all else fails, be grateful for all the things you do have and all the things you don't. And compare if you absolutely have to.

"Beauty cannot be perceived
but with a serene mind."
—*Henry David Thoreau*

What's the point of climbing to the top of a mountain to watch the sunrise if you're consumed by all that's wrong with your life? When you're in a moment that's designed to be appreciated, turn those thoughts off, or keep them at bay. Gently tell them that you will be with them in a second, you need a minute to enjoy this once-in-a-lifetime opportunity (which every moment is). You know those thoughts will be back, and if you're fearful you might lose a thought, write it down and put it in your pocket, so it will stop ruining your moment.

The heart is strong,
genuine, and authentic,
but
the mind is persistent,
pushy, and patient.

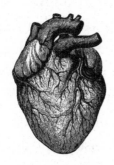 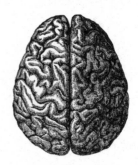

The mind makes a great tool, but a lousy master.

Marriage is not about compromise, *it's about sacrifice.* If you ever start keeping score, trying to figure out who's ahead of the game or who's making out better on the deal, stop that shit right away. Scorekeeping has no place in love, unless you're trying to make sure that the other person is getting the better end of the deal.

Don't get a tattoo
to cover up a bruise.

A problem cannot exist without a solution.

The only reason you feel the existence of a problem is because there is a solution that hasn't been applied yet. When this happens, sometimes action is the key, but usually acceptance will open the door to a solution much quicker and with much less effort.

True self-awareness can best be described this way:

You think you're behind the 8-ball, but you're actually way ahead of the curve. The people I've met that were the best at living life constantly thought they were behind, when in actuality, they were way ahead.

There's nothing worse than feeling like your body and your heart belong to two different people.

Expectations are resentments waiting to happen.

When I say that I expect very little or have low expectations, I don't mean that I expect bad things to happen. I mean I literally expect nothing.

Life comes as it comes, and I trust myself to handle the waves as they roll in.

There are certain things in this life that cannot be earned, only accepted (like grace).

That which cannot be understood, must be accepted. For instance, death must be accepted, because losing people is a motherfucker.

If I get frustrated when people vent to me, I'm not frustrated that they're in pain.
I'm frustrated that I can't do anything about it.

There's one surefire way to
stop advancing in your field:
Get too good at your job.
Too good to ask questions,
    too good to ask for help when
        you're overwhelmed,
and too proud to take advice from
    somebody with less experience
    and more enthusiasm than you.

It's infinitely better to *respond* than to *react*.

If "what doesn't kill you makes you stronger" is true, it also means you are the absolute strongest you've ever been at this moment in your life.

You can't prepare yourself intellectually for an emotional experience.

I remember when my grandmother was dying. I had done all I could do to pre-accept her passing, even wishing it for her so she could be done with the suffering. But none of that mattered when she actually died. I was devastated. I learned to appreciate the time I still have with people, rather than trying to prepare myself for life without them. It doesn't work.

So many times I thought I had discovered the key to life.

I finally realized that I would never discover a solitary key: that instead, discovery *was* the key.

A lot of people justify
their unhealthy behavior
by labeling it "normal."
  Just because something is normal
        doesn't mean that it's okay.

Watching somebody you care about stay in an abusive relationship is like watching a caged animal just sit there in front of the open door, paralyzed by fear of what's outside the cage.

It's not comfortable or free, but at least the discomfort is familiar.

There's perverse comfort in discomfort.

A few years ago, somebody gave me a piece of dating advice.

They said to make a list of everything I could ever want in a woman. Everything from physical characteristics to intensity of spiritual pursuit and all that falls in between. My list was comprised of about 60 items ranging from big boobs to must be a Jay-Z fan (or at least be willing to listen to me talk about Jay-Z). I read them all off, and when I finished, I just felt exasperated. I said, "I feel like nobody is going to ever squeeze into this ridiculously tight space I've created for somebody to fit." Realizing I was being dramatic, I corrected myself and said, "Okay, maybe not nobody, but it's going to be very hard to find." My friend exclaimed, "That's the point! It's supposed to be a hard position to fill!"

All you have to do to be funny
is say what everybody else is
thinking before they say it.
It works every time.
The trick is to condition yourself
to speak fast and think even
faster, but don't be weird.
Otherwise, people won't laugh;
they'll be scared, and it'll get
really awkward really fast.

I don't give a shit what people think of me.

If people don't like me, I genuinely feel bad for them, not because I'm this awesome guy that they're missing out on, but because *I know what it feels like to dislike someone.* I know what it feels like to walk in a room and see somebody I can't stand or I've been avoiding.

It feels like shit.

I don't like the fact that people feel that when they see me, but I don't like the fact that people feel that when they see anybody.

But if it has to be somebody, it may as well be me, because I can handle it.

Yes, you have free will, but *so does everybody else.*

Remember that when you feel like doing whatever the fuck you want without having to think of how it might affect other people.

I worked with a girl at a restaurant and one day she said something so negative, I had to pipe up. "Why are you so negative?" I asked.

"I'm not negative, I just state the obvious."

I had to challenge her. "Did you ever stop to think that what's so obvious to you is negativity because you've spent your entire life looking for it?"

She paused.

I paused.

And we never spoke of it again.

People who were raised to
be negative by negative people
spend their entire lives looking
for shit to be negative about
so they don't feel so weird
being negative all the time.
But the same also goes for joy. The
more joy you seek out, the more
you'll find and the more you'll feel.
Perception is a skill just like
anything else. The more you
practice it, the better you get.

Be gentle but firm with
your internal dialogue.
Don't yell at yourself, but don't cut
yourself too much slack either.
If you yell at yourself to get shit
done, you wind up fighting with
whatever version of yourself
that's doing the yelling.
And if you yell at yourself,
you won't like yourself.
Nobody likes to be yelled at,
especially by themselves.

In therapy, I was taught that I was going to have to re-parent myself due to the lack of supervision and guidance in my childhood. The first time I tried this self-parenting, I was about to call an ex-girlfriend I definitely should not have been calling. As I went to dial her number, it occurred to me that this would be a good time to re-parent myself.

Immediately, in my head, I started saying, "You dumb piece of shit, you're gonna call that fucking girl? Good move, idiot. Really fucking smart." Now, my parents didn't speak to me like this, but this was my idea of parenting for whatever reason, and it was exhausting. Worse, it made me feel terrible, and I shut down for the rest of the day. If a parent were to speak like that to a child, it would be called abuse. So don't do it to yourself.

People are born knowing
the difference between
right and wrong.
It's the job of the parents, teachers,
and friends to teach children the
ability to hear and honor that
inner voice whispering the right
choices during difficult times.

Void-filling behaviors must be curbed.

The void is a thing inside you that tells you you're not going to be complete until you have enough of "this" or you do enough of "that."

The void is the space between where you are and where you think you should be.

The problem is that when you feed the void, the void grows.

And the bigger it gets, the more it needs to eat.

Don't tell me some negative
shit and then tell me
you're being a "realist."
  I'm a realist, too, but the way I see
it, everything's pretty fucking good.

If you're gonna project into the future, at least project positive.
It never ceases to amaze me that when people think about the future, it's almost always negative.

The more honest you are
with yourself and other people,
the more you feel like you're
a part of the human race.

People keep secrets all the time,
either because they're embarrassed,
they think nobody cares, or they
don't know that everybody is
dealing with basically the same
issues, because everybody else
is keeping it a secret too.

If you're going to choose one "E" for the rest of your life, choose Effort.

The polar opposite of Effort is Expectations.

But if you can't choose one, because you're an imperfect human being like me, just know that Effort coupled with Expectations is infinitely better than Expectations with no Effort.

I have no self-control once
the food is in my house.
All my self-control is in
the supermarket.
If I don't bring shit food
home, *I can't eat it.*

"Move a muscle, change a thought."
This is a tool you can use when your mind is working against you and you can't seem to stop it. You have to move first, and let your mind follow. When I was dating this girl Jessica, I used to obsess over when and how quickly she called me or texted me back. One night in particular I was waiting for her to get off her shift at the restaurant she worked at. I knew beforehand that she comes home smelling like Greek food, but that didn't occur to me when she told me she left work, and I started to lose it. I laid on my bed, waiting and watching TV. The whole thing couldn't have taken more than 10 minutes, but I was on edge. I couldn't stop thinking about what she was doing, who she was with, and anything else bad that might have happened to her. My mind racing, I got up out of bed to move my muscles and change my thoughts. Within three seconds of getting out of my bed, I looked across the hallway and saw the bathroom door wide open, the shower curtain peeking out from behind it. "She's in the fucking shower you moron." I said to myself. She called me back soon after that, and as it turns out, she was in the shower. She wasn't banging her ex-boyfriend as I suspected.

When I feel like the world is going to hell in a handbasket, it's actually just my perspective that's going to hell.

Ten percent of people are nasty to nice people.

Eighty percent of people are nice to nice people.

Ten percent of people are nice to nasty people.

The more I find myself in that latter group, the better off my life seems to be. That doesn't mean I eat shit and let people walk all over me (I'm hardly a pushover), but if you're gonna be a dick, you have to deal with that. If I'm a dick back to you, I have to deal with that, and to be honest, nobody is worth my sanity.

It's not good to surround yourself with only like-minded people.

Of course it's easier and there's less friction, but where's the growth in that? Make it a point to be around people that you disagree with on topics near and dear to both of you. It's important to you for a reason, and the same goes for them. They have a reason they feel the way they do, and it's good for you to hear what that reason is. Don't ever assume that somebody is stupid because they share a different opinion than you do. And don't assume somebody is smart because they share an opinion you have.

Smart people simplify complicated things and
stupid people complicate
simple things.

Everybody has baggage.
You just have to find somebody
who's willing to help you carry
yours, and someone whose
baggage you will happily carry.

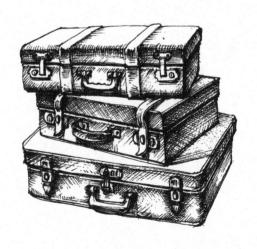

Marriage is not the end
of the search for love.
It's the end of the search
for the person to love.
The search for ways to love
that person has *just begun.*

CPSIA information can be obtained
at www.ICGtesting.com
Printed in the USA
BVOW03s1537171217
503017BV00001B/8/P